Polar Animals

Puffins

by Helen Frost

Consulting Editor: Gail Saunders-Smith, PhD

Consultant: Brian M. Barnes, Director
Institute of Arctic Biology
University of Alaska, Fairbanks

Capstone press®

Mankato, Minnesota

Pebble Books are published by Capstone Press,
151 Good Counsel Drive, P.O. Box 669, Mankato, Minnesota 56002.
www.capstonepress.com

1 2 3 4 5 6 11 10 09 08 07 06

Library of Congress Cataloging-in-Publication Data
Frost, Helen, 1949–
    Puffins / by Helen Frost.
        p. cm.—(Pebble books. Polar animals)
    Summary: "Simple text and photographs present puffins, where they live, and
what they do"—Provided by publisher.
    Includes bibliographical references (p. 23) and index.
    ISBN-13: 978-0-7368-4244-0 (hardcover)
    ISBN-10: 0-7368-4244-6 (hardcover)
    1. Puffins—Juvenile literature. I. Title. II. Series: Polar Animals.
QL696.C42F76 2007
598.3'3—dc22   2004026896

Note to Parents and Teachers

The Polar Animals set supports national science standards related to
life science. This book describes and illustrates puffins. The images
support early readers in understanding the text. The repetition of
words and phrases helps early readers learn new words. This book
also introduces early readers to subject-specific vocabulary words,
which are defined in the Glossary section. Early readers may need
assistance to read some words and to use the Table of Contents,
Glossary, Read More, Internet Sites, and Index sections of the book.

Table of Contents

What Are Puffins? 5
Where Puffins Live 7
Body Parts 11
What Puffins Do 17

Glossary 22
Read More 23
Internet Sites 23
Index 24

4

What Are Puffins?

Puffins are black
and white seabirds.
Puffins have
large, colorful beaks.

land where puffins live

other areas where puffins live

Where Puffins Live

Puffins live in cold northern areas. They spend most of their lives alone on the ocean.

7

In summer, puffins nest
in large colonies.
They gather
on sea cliffs.

Body Parts

Puffins have short wings.
They use their wings
to fly and swim.

Puffins have orange legs
and webbed feet.
They use their feet
to steer in the water.

Puffins have short feathers.
The feathers trap air
to help puffins float.

What Puffins Do

Puffins dive
and swim underwater.
They push air out
of their feathers
when they dive.

Puffins eat small fish.
They catch fish
with their sharp beaks.

Puffins can carry many
fish in their beaks.
They bring the fish
back to their young.

Glossary

beak—the hard part of a bird's mouth

cliff—a high, steep rock face

colony—a large group of birds that live together; puffins live in colonies while they are nesting and raising their young.

dive—to plunge underwater

feather—one of the light fluffy parts that cover a bird's body

nest—to build a place to lay eggs and bring up young; puffins lay one egg a year.

seabird—a bird that lives near the ocean

steer—to guide or direct

webbed—having a fold of skin or tissue that connects the toes

Read More

Lindeen, Carol K. *Life in a Polar Region.* Living in a Biome. Mankato, Minn.: Capstone Press, 2004.

McMillan, Bruce. *Puffins Climb, Penguins Rhyme.* San Diego: Harcourt Brace, 2001.

Internet Sites

FactHound offers a safe, fun way to find Internet sites related to this book. All of the sites on FactHound have been researched by our staff.

Here's how:

1. Visit *www.facthound.com*

2. Choose your grade level.

3. Type in this book ID **0736842446** for age-appropriate sites. You may also browse subjects by clicking on letters, or by clicking on pictures and words.

4. Click on the **Fetch It** button.

FactHound will fetch the best sites for you!

Index

beaks, 5, 19, 21
colonies, 9
color, 5, 13
diving, 17
feathers, 15, 17
fish, 19, 21

floating, 15
flying, 11
food, 19, 21
legs, 13
nesting, 9
ocean, 7
seabirds, 5
sea cliffs, 9

steering, 13
summer, 9
swimming, 11, 17
webbed feet, 13
wings, 11
young, 21

Word Count: 121
Grade: 1
Early-Intervention Level: 14

Editorial Credits

Martha E. H. Rustad and Rebecca Stromstad Glaser, editors; Patrick D. Dentinger, designer; Wanda Winch, photo researcher; Scott Thoms, photo editor

Photo Credits

Bruce Coleman Inc./John Shaw, 8; Robert Falls Sr., 12
Eyewire (Photodisc), 20
Minden Pictures/Foto Natura/Flip De Nooyer, 14; Frans Lanting, 16; Michio Hoshino, 6
Robert McCaw, 4, 18
SuperStock/age fotostock, cover
Unicorn Stock Photos/Robert E. Barber, 10
U.S. Fish & Wildlife Service, 1